CORE LIBRARY OF US STATES

TEXAS

BY TAMMY GAGNE

CONTENT CONSULTANT
Brennan Rivas, PhD
Texas Historian

Core Library

An Imprint of Abdo Publishing
abdobooks.com

abdobooks.com

Published by Abdo Publishing, a division of ABDO, PO Box 398166, Minneapolis, Minnesota 55439.

Printed in the United States of America, North Mankato, Minnesota.
052022
092022

THIS BOOK CONTAINS RECYCLED MATERIALS

Cover Photos: Shutterstock Images, (map and icons), (cow), (butterflies), (peppers), (flower)
Interior Photos: Dean Fikar/iStockphoto, 4–5, 43; Red Line Editorial, 7 (Texas), 7 (USA); iStockphoto, 10, 12 (bird), 12 (dog), 12 (butterfly); Rosemary Woller/Shutterstock Images, 10–11; T. Lesia/Shutterstock Images, 12 (flag); Brian Luke/Shutterstock Images, 12 (flower); World History Archive/Alamy, 16; Stuart Villanueva/Galveston County Daily News/AP Images, 18; Linda Moon/Shutterstock Images, 22–23, 45; Matt Jeppson/Shutterstock Images, 27; Roschetzky Photography/Shutterstock Images, 28–29; Wangkun Jia/Shutterstock Images, 32; Delcia Lopez/Monitor/AP Images, 34–35; FPG/Hulton Archive/Archive Photos/Getty Images, 39; Robert Waltman/iStockphoto, 40

Editor: Angela Lim
Series Designer: Joshua Olson

Library of Congress Control Number: 2021951547

Publisher's Cataloging-in-Publication Data

Names: Gagne, Tammy, author.
Title: Texas / by Tammy Gagne
Description: Minneapolis, Minnesota : Abdo Publishing, 2023 | Series: Core library of US states | Includes online resources and index.
Identifiers: ISBN 9781532197857 (lib. bdg.) | ISBN 9781098270612 (ebook)
Subjects: LCSH: U.S. states--Juvenile literature. | Southwestern States--Juvenile literature. | Texas--History--Juvenile literature. | Physical geography--United States--Juvenile literature.
Classification: DDC 976.4--dc23

Population demographics broken down by race and ethnicity come from the 2019 census estimate. Population totals come from the 2020 census.

CONTENTS

CHAPTER ONE
The Lone Star State 4

CHAPTER TWO
History of Texas 10

CHAPTER THREE
Geography and Climate 22

CHAPTER FOUR
Resources and Economy 28

CHAPTER FIVE
People and Places 34

Important Dates 42

Stop and Think 44

Glossary 46

Online Resources 47

Learn More 47

Index 48

About the Author 48

CHAPTER ONE

THE LONE STAR STATE

The warm San Antonio wind blows gently as tourists gather at the Alamo. This was the site of one of the most famous battles in US history. Texas once belonged to Mexico. Texas fought for its independence from that nation in the Texas Revolution (1835–1836). The Alamo was a battle site during this war. Today the tourists look up at a flag flying over the former military fort. The flag is red, white, and blue with a single white star. That lone star is a powerful

In 1718 Spanish missionaries founded Mission San Antonio de Valero. This building would later be named the Alamo.

symbol of Texas's hard fight for its freedom. It is where Texas got its nickname, the Lone Star State.

PERSPECTIVES

MORE THAN FARMS

Some people who have never visited Texas think it's mostly made up of ranches and farms. Television shows and movies often support this stereotype. Many feature cowboys and their horses. Texas has its share of rural areas. But the state also has many large cities. Some visitors are surprised when they see the skyscrapers that paint the landscapes of these busy urban areas. Singer Beyoncé grew up in Houston. She has said, "When I describe Houston to friends who have never been here, I first have to tell them, no, it's not like the country films you see on TV!"

EVERYTHING IS BIGGER IN TEXAS

Texans have a saying that everything is bigger in Texas. It is the second-largest US state in area. It's the most populated state in the South. It also has the most farms in the nation. These sprawling farms grow much of the country's food. In addition to its vast land, Texas is also known for

MAP OF TEXAS

Texas is a large state. How does this map help you understand the cities and natural features Texas has to offer?

its abundance of oil. It produces the most oil of any US state.

Texas borders four US states and Mexico. Arkansas and Louisiana lie to the east. Oklahoma forms Texas's northern border. New Mexico borders Texas to the west. Mexico borders the south. This border follows the river named Rio Grande. The Gulf of Mexico lies to the southeast of the state. The gulf is connected to the Caribbean Sea.

Texas's largest city is Houston. It has a population of more than 2.3 million. Other large cities in the state include San Antonio, Dallas, and Austin. Many people call San Antonio the Alamo City because it is the home of the legendary fort. The Dallas Zoo is one of the most popular zoos in the country. Austin has been the capital city since 1839. These cities and many others are bustling business centers for some of the nation's most successful companies. ExxonMobil and AT&T are just two of the companies with headquarters in Texas.

People travel from all around the world to visit Texas. Tourists can explore historical sites such as the Alamo or spend a day at Space Center Houston. This site is the official visitor center of the National Aeronautics and Space Administration (NASA) Johnson Space Center. Outdoorsy visitors can venture into Big Bend National Park or Guadalupe Mountains National Park. No matter what type of interests visitors have, Texas is sure to offer something that matches their tastes.

TEXAS CHILI COOK-OFFS

Many Texans take pride in their chili-making skills. Chili cook-offs take place all over the state. Those who take part in these competitions call themselves chiliheads. They take the dish very seriously. Most chiliheads insist that a true Texan would never put beans in chili. But some use unusual ingredients, such as chocolate, coffee, and peanut butter.

CHAPTER TWO

HISTORY OF TEXAS

People have lived in Texas for more than 10,000 years. The first humans to arrive in the area were the Paleo-Indians. They were hunters and gatherers who traveled through the region to find food.

Thousands of years later, hundreds of American Indian nations occupied the land. These nations included the Apache nations, the Comanche (Nʉmʉnʉʉ), and the Wichita. These nations established different governments and cultures. For example the Karankawa traveled

Hueco Tanks State Park and Historic Site offers opportunities for hiking. Visitors can also see cave drawings, *inset*, made by early cultures.

TEXAS

QUICK FACTS

Take a look at the Texas state symbols and statistics. Was any of the information surprising? Why?

Abbreviation: TX
Nickname: The Lone Star State
Motto: Friendship
Date of statehood: December 29, 1845
Capital: Austin
Population: 29,145,505
Area: 268,596 square miles (695,660 sq km)

STATE SYMBOLS

State bird
Northern mockingbird

State flower
Bluebonnet

State dog
Blue Lacy

State insect
Monarch butterfly

to follow food supplies. The Caddo lived in permanent villages. Some of these peoples still live in Texas today.

SPANISH RULE

Mexico was part of the Spanish Empire in the late 1530s. At that time Spanish explorers traveled north and entered present-day Texas. They claimed the area for Spain. El Paso was established in 1682. It was the first permanent Spanish settlement in Texas.

Many American Indian peoples suffered under Spanish rule. They fought with the Spanish over land. The Spanish also carried diseases that killed millions of American Indian people.

After approximately 300 years under Spanish rule, Mexico fought with Spain in the Mexican War of Independence (1810–1821). Mexico defeated Spain, ending Spanish rule in the region. Mexico took over the land, which included Texas. The Texas region had been part of the Spanish Empire for hundreds of years. But many of the people living there were of Mexican descent. This allowed a unique culture to develop. Texans of Mexican descent are known as Tejanos.

THE REPUBLIC OF TEXAS

In the early 1800s, many of the people living in Texas were immigrants from the US South. They brought enslaved people with them. The US settlers quickly outnumbered the Tejanos. The Mexican government began to worry that the United States would take over Texas.

Over the years, the practices of the Mexican government began to shift. Mexico outlawed slavery in 1829. Texan farmers depended on enslaved laborers to run their farms. In 1833 Antonio López de Santa Anna became the president of Mexico. He created a new constitution for Mexico. Tensions began to rise between the Mexican government and some Mexican states, including Texas. The first battle in the Texas Revolution occurred in 1835.

Texas declared independence from Mexico on March 2, 1836. This led the Mexican army to attack the Alamo under the leadership of Santa Anna, who was a Mexican general at this time. The Mexican army killed every Texan army member. But the war wasn't over.

> **PERSPECTIVES**
>
> **SURVIVORS OF THE ALAMO**
>
> Susanna Wilkerson Dickinson was one of the Texans who survived the battle at the Alamo. Mexican soldiers found Dickinson and her baby in one of the Alamo rooms. They were hiding with other women and children. General Santa Anna questioned the women. He sent Dickinson to pass along a letter of warning to Sam Houston's army. Much of what is known about the battle at the Alamo comes from the accounts of Dickinson and the other survivors.

General Sam Houston led the Texas army to the banks of the San Jacinto River. Juan Seguín was with him. Seguín headed the only Tejano unit at San Jacinto. "Remember the Alamo!" became the rallying cry during the battle. The Texas army defeated the

Mexican army on April 21, 1836. The army captured Santa Anna. The Texas army and Santa Anna signed the Treaties of Velasco. Texas became its own country, the Republic of Texas. But Mexico did not recognize Texas's independence until 1848.

BECOMING A US STATE

After the Texas Revolution, US settlers became increasingly hostile to Mexicans and Tejanos. Many Tejanos left Texas for Mexico. US settlers and culture began to dominate Texas. As early as 1836, the majority of Texans wanted the region to become a US state. But the issue of slavery slowed Texas's entrance into the nation. Some Northern states did not want another slave state to join the Union. Texas eventually became the twenty-eighth state on December 29, 1845.

Soon after, President James K. Polk sent troops into Mexico. He wanted to expand US land and

Antonio López de Santa Anna was the Mexican general during the Texas Revolution. He also served as the president of Mexico 11 times over the course of 22 years.

Texans celebrated the dedication of a Juneteenth mural in Galveston in 2021. That year Juneteenth became a US holiday.

establish Texas's borders. This action led to the Mexican-American War (1846–1848). After the United States won the war, the Mexican government signed the Treaty of Guadalupe Hidalgo. This treaty gave the United States land in the Southwest and extended Texas's southern boundary to the Rio Grande.

The United States was soon heading toward another war. Northern states wanted to outlaw slavery. But Texas and other Southern states wanted to keep allowing it. Northern and Southern states clashed during the American Civil War (1861–1865). Southern states including Texas left the United States and formed a new nation where slavery was allowed. This country was called the Confederate States of America. Nearly 90,000 Texans served in the Confederate Army before the northern states of the Union won the war in 1865.

Major General Gordon Granger arrived in Galveston on June 19, 1865. He announced that enslaved people were free. People in Texas soon began celebrating the historic date. They named it Juneteenth, a combination of the words *June* and *Nineteenth*.

GOVERNMENT AND PRESIDENTS

The Texas government is made up of three branches. The governor leads the executive branch. Texas voters elect a governor. They also elect members to the

JOHN F. KENNEDY

On November 22, 1963, President John F. Kennedy and First Lady Jacqueline Kennedy were riding in an automobile parade through downtown Dallas. Three shots were fired at their vehicle. Two of the bullets hit the president. Half an hour later, medical staff at Parkland Memorial Hospital declared Kennedy dead. Later that day, Lee Harvey Oswald was arrested for the assassination. He was shot and killed while being taken to jail.

legislative branch, which makes laws. The Texas Supreme Court and lower courts form the judicial branch. This branch interprets laws. Texas also has three federally recognized American Indian tribes. They are the Alabama-Coushatta Tribe of Texas, the Kickapoo Traditional Tribe of Texas, and the Ysleta del Sur Pueblo. Each nation has its own government.

Texas has been home to many famous politicians. Lyndon B. Johnson became president in 1963. Barbara Jordan made history in 1966 when she became a

Texas senator. She was the first Black woman to hold office in a state senate.

Texans celebrated when George H. W. Bush was elected as the vice president of the United States in 1980 under President Ronald Reagan. Bush had moved to Texas with his family in 1950. Bush and Reagan served two terms together before Bush himself was elected president in 1988. Bush's son George W. Bush became president in 2000 and served two terms.

FURTHER EVIDENCE

Chapter Two discusses Texas's fight for independence. What was one of the main points? What evidence is included to support this point? Read the article at the website below. Does the information on the website support this point? Does it present new evidence?

THE REPUBLIC OF TEXAS

abdocorelibrary.com/texas

CHAPTER THREE

GEOGRAPHY AND CLIMATE

Texas has many types of terrain, including more than 40 mountain ranges. Guadalupe Peak is the highest point in Texas. It stands 8,749 feet (2,667 m) above sea level.

Forests cover approximately 38 percent of Texas. Big Thicket National Preserve is the largest. The preserve includes clearings with spectacular views of trees, waterways, and wildlife.

The Rio Grande forms the southern border of Texas and flows through Big Bend National Park.

Approximately 12 percent of Texas is desert. The Chihuahuan Desert is the largest desert in North America. It extends from Mexico and reaches into Arizona, New Mexico, and southwestern Texas.

Most of the remaining land consists of prairies and other grasslands. Many waterways also flow through Texas. The longest is the Rio Grande. It stretches from Colorado to the Gulf of Mexico.

CLIMATE AND WEATHER

Climate varies throughout the large state. Eastern Texas is more humid than western Texas. Winters are generally cool, while summers can get quite hot. Temperatures are generally colder in the north. Two northern cities tied for the coldest temperature on record for the state. Tulia and Seminole have dropped to −23 degrees Fahrenheit (−31°C). But it gets hot in the north too. In 1994 the city of Monahans reached 120 degrees Fahrenheit (49°C).

Precipitation also varies greatly. The northern panhandle gets the most snow. Up to 30 inches (76 cm) falls each year. Eastern Texas gets rain instead. This area receives as much as 60 inches (152 cm) annually, more rainfall than any other area in the state.

Hurricanes, droughts, and tornadoes often strike the state. A severe drought known as the Dust Bowl occurred in western Texas in the mid-1930s. High winds blew dry soil through the air. The drought made it difficult to grow food, forcing thousands of families to leave the area.

PERSPECTIVES

HURRICANE HARVEY

Hurricane Harvey struck Texas on August 25, 2017. Sixty-eight Texans died as a direct result of the hurricane. Strong winds and floodwaters caused approximately $125 billion in damage. Iashia Nelson and her family were living in Houston when the hurricane hit. Two years after the storm, she shared how the hurricane continues to affect her son. She said, "If it's raining really hard, he'd be like, 'We have to move, it's gonna flood.' You know, he's still terrified."

TEXAS BLIND SALAMANDER

Texas was home to 147 endangered species in 2020. One is the Texas blind salamander. This salamander doesn't have eyes. It hunts by sensing the movement of other animals in the water. The Texas blind salamander lives only in underwater caves near San Marcos. Pollution and city growth threaten this animal. It needs clean waters to survive.

PLANTS AND ANIMALS

Texas is home to more than 2,700 types of wildflowers, including bluebonnets, which are Texas's state flower. Wildflowers attract insects and butterflies. More than 400 butterfly species are found in Texas. Among them is the state insect, the monarch butterfly. Monarchs fly over Texas as they migrate from the United States to Mexico for the winter.

Big Thicket National Preserve is known for its wildlife. The northern mockingbird is just one of the 74 types of birds that live there. The preserve is also home to plants that trap and digest insects for energy, such as pitcher plants.

The Texas horned lizard is the state reptile of Texas.

Other types of plants and animals live in Texas deserts. Yucca and prickly pear cacti can survive with little water. Unique animals such as the nine-banded armadillo and the Texas horned lizard also live in dry areas.

EXPLORE ONLINE

Chapter Three discusses the migration of monarch butterflies through Texas. The website below focuses on the same topic. As you know, every source is different. How is the information at the website different from the information in this chapter? What information is the same? What information did you learn from the website?

MONARCH BUTTERFLIES STOP BY TEXAS DURING MIGRATION TO CENTRAL MEXICO

abdocorelibrary.com/texas

CHAPTER FOUR

RESOURCES AND ECONOMY

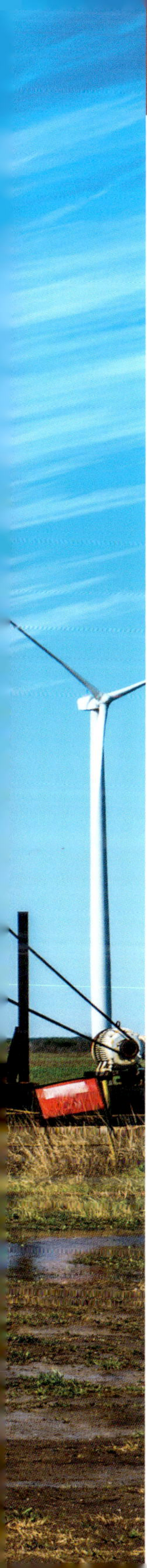

Texas has a long history of oil production. Its first oil well was established in 1866. By the early 1900s, the state was producing more than 17 million barrels each year. Oil and gas remain important parts of the Texas economy. As much as 35 percent of the state's revenue comes from these products. But oil spills also happen in Texas every year. These accidents hurt wildlife and damage the environment.

Texas is the largest energy-producing and energy-consuming US state.

PERSPECTIVES

THE DEEPWATER HORIZON OIL SPILL

In 2010 an explosion occurred on the Deepwater Horizon oil rig off the Texas coast. The explosion killed 11 people. Millions of gallons of oil spilled into the Gulf of Mexico, causing severe damage to wildlife. Tourism and fishing industries also suffered. In 2021 US Secretary of the Interior Deb Haaland spoke of the spill. She wanted to make sure this type of event did not happen again. Haaland said, "The lives and livelihoods of Gulf Coast workers and communities . . . and the future of our ocean and waters depend on our action."

Texas is also a leader in renewable energy. The state is first in the nation in wind energy production. Texas is also one of the top producers of solar energy in the United States. In 2020 it ranked second only to California.

FARMING AND RANCHING

Texas farmers grow much of the nation's food. Corn, wheat, pecans, and citrus fruits are just a few of the state's crops. More than 98 percent of Texas farms are still run by individuals or families.

Ranching is also widespread in Texas. Cattle ranches bring more than $12 billion to the state's economy each year. The Texas longhorn is bred on many Texas ranches.

TEXAS TOURISM

Tourism is one of the most important industries in Texas. People travel to Texas to visit the state's cities and national parks. It recorded more than 72.5 million out-of-state visitors in 2018. That year more than 1.2 million Texans worked in the tourism industry. This includes jobs in hotels, restaurants, and transportation. In 2019 tourism brought approximately $169 billion into the state.

TECHNOLOGY AND SPACE

Many of the nation's top companies have factories in Texas. The technology company Dell was founded in Austin. It brings more than $90 billion a year to the Texas economy. Dell has factories around the world. But the company still has facilities in six Texas cities.

The Johnson Space Center has models of important space vehicles, including the space shuttle *Endeavour*.

The Johnson Space Center in Houston is where NASA astronauts train. The center was established in 1961. It was first called the Manned Spacecraft Center. It was renamed in 1973 to honor the late president Lyndon B. Johnson. The Johnson Space Center is also home to Mission Control. This is the part of NASA that manages flights to and from space. Today Johnson Space Center employs 52,000 people. The center partners with many research universities. Popular movies about space travel, including *Apollo 13*, *First Man*, and *The Martian*, have had scenes that were filmed at the Johnson Space Center.

STRAIGHT TO THE SOURCE

In 2018 Texas Governor Greg Abbott wrote an opinion piece featured on CNBC. He described Texas's economic success:

> *The Texas economy is the fastest growing in the nation. More Texans are working than ever before as the Lone Star State leads in private-sector job creation. . . . And jobs in Texas are now on pace for the strongest growth in four years. . . .*
>
> *But more than the bounty of land, our greatest natural resource in Texas is our . . . workforce. It's why Texas is . . . the top state for jobs created by foreign and domestic investment. In fact, when you combine all goods and services produced by the people and businesses in the Lone Star State, [Texas's economy is] the 10th-largest among the nations of the world.*

Source: Greg Abbott. "Why Texas Is the Top State for Business in America." *Office of the Texas Governor*, 12 July 2018, gov.texas.gov. Accessed 15 June 2021.

BACK IT UP

The author of this passage is using evidence to support a point. Write a paragraph describing the point the author is making. Then write down two or three pieces of evidence the author uses to make the point.

CHAPTER FIVE

PEOPLE AND PLACES

Approximately 29 million people call Texas home. They come from a variety of places and celebrate different cultures. More than 41 percent of Texans are non-Hispanic white. People who are Hispanic or Latino make up nearly 40 percent of the population. Approximately 13 percent of Texans are Black, 5 percent are Asian, and 1 percent are American Indian.

Texas has also developed its own culture. Tejanos have helped shape this culture,

Traditional Mexican cultures are celebrated at the Shah Calenda Parade in McAllen.

which is reflected in arts, music, and Tex-Mex cuisine. Texas rodeos, chili, and barbecue all have roots in Tejano culture.

Cultural celebrations take place all over Texas. The Tops in Texas Rodeo is held in Jacksonville. Spectators watch rodeo athletes compete in activities such as bull riding, calf roping, and barrel racing. Another popular event is the Houston Latin Fest. This annual festival celebrates Latin culture with a strong focus on Latin art, food, and music.

CELEBRITIES FROM TEXAS

Many famous people are proud to hail from Texas. Actress and singer Selena Gomez was born in Grand Prairie. She grew up in nearby Dallas. Actor Matthew McConaughey was born in Uvalde. This small city lies about 80 miles (129 km) west of San Antonio.

Patrick Mahomes II was born in Tyler, Texas. He went on to play for Texas Tech University before being drafted into the National Football League. Music artists

Beyoncé and Kenny Rogers were both born in Houston.

SPORTS AND OTHER ATTRACTIONS

Professional sports are popular in Texas. The state has two football teams, the Dallas Cowboys and the Houston Texans. Texas is also home to two baseball teams. The Astros play in Houston, and the Rangers' home field is in Arlington. Basketball fans in Texas have even more teams to follow. The Dallas Mavericks, Houston Rockets, and San Antonio Spurs are all part of the National

PERSPECTIVES

THE GIFT OF MUSIC

Country music superstar Maren Morris grew up in Arlington. She began singing at fairs when she was just 11. By the time she was a teenager, Morris was performing at clubs and dance halls all over the state. She moved to Nashville, Tennessee, right before her big break. But she never forgot all the gifts that her home state gave her. She has said, "I was so fortunate to be brought up in a state where they had a music scene, because a lot of my friends here in Nashville . . . had to move here just to find one."

WHAT IS A TEXAS RANGER?

The Texas Rangers baseball team is named after a military law enforcement unit. The group formed in the 1830s. The Rangers served in the region while Texans fought for independence from Mexico. In 1935 they merged with the Texas Highway Patrol. Today the Texas Rangers remain a part of the Texas Department of Public Safety. They often lead investigations of major crimes.

Basketball Association. The Dallas Wings are part of the Women's National Basketball Association.

Texas offers many other attractions. Guadalupe Mountains National Park has deserts, canyons, and mountains. Visitors to Big Bend National Park can enjoy spending time on the banks of the Rio Grande. Both parks have many hiking trails. People who prefer milder terrain often enjoy visiting San Antonio's River Walk. Visitors can take in its great views

Texas Rangers Benjamin Maney Gault, *left*, and Frank Hamer, *right*, helped catch the famous outlaws Clyde Barrow and Bonnie Parker.

El Capitan is a famous peak in Guadalupe Mountains National Park.

while dining at restaurants, listening to live music, or staying at one of the many hotels along the walk.

Texas is a state that is rich in history, natural resources, and entertainment. People can choose from a variety of fun activities. They can visit locations throughout the state and experience all that Texas has to offer.

STRAIGHT TO THE SOURCE

Journalist Andrew Evans traveled to Big Bend National Park. In an article about his trip, he wrote:

> *Standing alone on the shattered ground of the Chihuahuan desert, where the sun bakes my neck and the wind breathes hot air onto my face, I truly know that I have arrived in Texas. Nothing smells quite like the desert, especially in March, when the bluebonnets are wide open and blowing their perfume across the dusty expanse—and nothing compares to the wild colored mountains of Big Bend.*

Source: Andrew Evans. "Big Bend National Park." *National Geographic*, 11 Mar. 2013, nationalgeographic.com. Accessed 15 June 2021.

WHAT'S THE BIG IDEA?

Take a close look at Evans's words. What is his main idea? What evidence is used to support his point? Write a few sentences showing how Evans uses two or three pieces of evidence to support his main point.

IMPORTANT DATES

10,000 years ago
Paleo-Indians live in the area now known as Texas.

1682
The first Spanish settlement in Texas is established in El Paso.

1821
Spanish rule of Mexico ends. Texas is part of Mexico at this time.

1835
The Texas Revolution begins.

1836
Texans suffer a devastating loss at the Alamo. The Texas army later defeats the Mexican army. General Antonio López de Santa Anna signs the Treaties of Velasco. Texas becomes an independent country, the Republic of Texas.

1845
Texas becomes the twenty-eighth US state on December 29.

1865
Major General Gordon Granger arrives in Galveston and announces the end of slavery on June 19.

1963
President John F. Kennedy is assassinated in Dallas on November 22.

2010
Eleven workers die and millions of gallons of oil spill into the Gulf of Mexico after an explosion on the Deepwater Horizon oil rig.

STOP AND THINK

Tell the Tale

Chapter One discusses a trip to the Alamo. Imagine that you are taking a tour of the historic site. Write 200 words about your experience. Describe what you see and hear, as well as how you feel standing at the site of such an important event in history.

Surprise Me

This book discusses the history of Texas. After reading this book, what two or three facts about Texas history did you find most surprising? Write a few sentences about each fact. Why did you find each fact surprising?

Take a Stand

Texas's oil industry has a large effect on the economy and environment. The oil industry creates jobs and brings billions of dollars to the Texas economy. But accidents that cause oil spills can harm natural wildlife. Do you think the benefits of oil outweigh the risks? Or do you think the risks are too high?

Another View

This book talks about Juneteenth. As you know, every source is different. Ask an adult to help you find another source about this national holiday. Write a short essay comparing and contrasting the new source's point of view with that of this book's author. What is the point of view of each source? How are they similar and why? How are they different and why?

GLOSSARY

assassination
the killing of an important person, often for political reasons

endangered species
a type of animal or plant that is at risk of dying out completely

immigrant
a person who moves to and lives in a new country

migrate
to move to a different location, usually as the seasons change

panhandle
a narrow strip of land that is shaped like the handle of a pan when viewed on a map

revenue
income from the sales or services of an industry, a company, or an individual

stereotype
a general, oversimplified idea about a place or group of people

thicket
a dense group of trees

ONLINE RESOURCES

To learn more about Texas, visit our free resource websites below.

Core Library CONNECTION
FREE! COMMON CORE MULTIMEDIA RESOURCES

Visit **abdocorelibrary.com** or scan this QR code for free Common Core resources for teachers and students, including vetted activities, multimedia, and booklinks, for deeper subject comprehension.

Booklinks NONFICTION NETWORK
FREE! ONLINE NONFICTION RESOURCES

Visit **abdobooklinks.com** or scan this QR code for free additional online weblinks for further learning. These links are routinely monitored and updated to provide the most current information available.

LEARN MORE

Ryan, Todd. *Houston Texans*. Abdo, 2020.

Ryckman, Tatiana. *Texas: The Lone Star State*. Cavendish Square, 2020.

Stanborough, Rebecca. *Exploring the South*. Abdo, 2018.

INDEX

agriculture, 6, 14, 30–31
Alamo, 5, 8–9, 15
American Indians, 11, 13, 20, 35

Beyoncé, 6, 37
Big Bend National Park, 7, 9, 38, 41
Big Thicket National Preserve, 7, 23, 26

chilis, 9, 36
Civil War, 19

Dallas, 7, 8, 20, 36–38

Houston, 6, 7, 8–9, 25, 32, 36–37
hurricanes, 25

Johnson Space Center, 9, 32
Juneteenth, 19

Kennedy, John F., 20

Mexico, 5, 8, 13–18, 24, 26–27, 38
monarch butterflies, 12, 26–27
mountains, 7, 9, 23, 38, 41

oil, 8, 29, 30

Rio Grande, 7, 8, 18, 24, 38

San Antonio, 5, 7, 8, 36–38
slavery, 14, 17, 19
Spain, 13
sports, 37–38

technology, 31
Tejanos, 14–17, 35–36
Texas Rangers, 37, 38
tourism, 5, 9, 30, 31
Treaty of Guadalupe Hidalgo, 18

wildlife, 26–27

About the Author

Tammy Gagne has written hundreds of books for both adults and children. Some of her recent books have been about media literacy and mental health. She lives in northern New England with her husband, son, and several pets.